MY COLLECTED RECIPES

FROM GENERATION TO GENERATION

MY COLLECTED RECIPES

Edited by Phoebe Lloyd
and Sheila Schwartz

First Published by
Octopus Books Inc.
645 Fifth Avenue
New York, N.Y. 10022

Copyright © 1979 Kimberly Publications, Inc.

Produced by Kimberly Publications, Inc.
Redding Ridge, Connecticut 06876
Printed in the United States of America

ISBN 7064 1164 1   Library of Congress Card No. 78-70930

Printed and bound in the United States of America

These Recipes and Menus are Dedicated To:

This Cookbook was compiled by:

and started on

Table of Contents

Introduction	6
SPECIAL RECIPES	10
Specialties of the House	12
Heirloom Recipes	18
Fast Main Dish Recipes	22
Children's Favorite Recipes	26
MENUS	30
Breakfast	32
Brunch	34
Lunch	36
Coffee or Tea Break	38
Dinner	40
Snacks	42
Parties	44
Barbecues & Picnics	46
Special Occasions	48
Holiday Specialties	50
Memorable Meals I Have Served	54
RECIPES	58
Hors d'oeuvres	60
Appetizers	64
Soups	66
Salads & Salad Dressings	70
Vegetables	74
Meats	78
Poultry	86
Fish	90
Casseroles	94

Sauces & Gravies 96
Egg Dishes & Soufflés 98
Breads & Rolls 102
DESSERTS & BEVERAGES 106
Desserts 108
Favorite Wines 114
Beverages 116
Favorite Cheeses 120
Preserves & Condiments 124
REFERENCE 128
Herbs & Spices 130
Calorie Counter 132
Favorite Cookbooks 142
Metric Conversion Charts 144
Weights & Measures (& Oven Temperatures) 148
Ingredients Substitution 150
Glossary of Cooking Terms 151
Personal Index 152
Guest Lists 154

Introduction

The cookbook that now has such a common place in everyone's kitchen did not always exist. In fact the first cookbooks, published over two thousand years ago, had no recipes! Instead of giving cooking directions, the ancient Greeks and Romans wrote poems about the philosophy of food—about how different dishes affected the guests' temperaments, or what to serve at a glorious banquet. Later, during the Middle Ages, written recipes appeared only in herbals or health handbooks, their purpose being to instruct the reader about the medicinal benefits of herbs, spices, plants, and vegetables. A typical medieval "recipe" describes spinach as a cure for coughs and other chest ailments. It is prepared by taking "leaves still wet with rain water and frying them with vinegar or aromatic herbs." For people not suffering from respiratory diseases, there were of course more appetizing ways of cooking spinach. But these recipes were passed on from generation to generation by word of mouth. Every professional cook took on apprentices, who trained for years before going out on their own or succeeding their masters. In short, the art of cooking remained so strongly within the oral tradition that no one thought to commit recipes to paper.

One look at the cooking section of any bookstore shows how much things have changed. Today, cookbooks exist in the thousands, with hundreds of new ones published every year. They provide recipes for everything from simple, homestyle fare to the most exotic cuisine. And even though such cookbooks can be extremely useful, their sheer number is sometimes overwhelming. Moreover, they are written for many people, not for you as

an individual. So you usually go through a cookbook and select those recipes that suit your personal tastes and needs, and or varying them for your own kitchen.

How do you keep track of the recipes you have tried and liked? Perhaps you copy them out and file them away in little boxes, put marks in the appropriate pages of the cookbook, or just hope you'll remember where to find that great recipe when you need it again. This book provides a unique opportunity to give your favorite recipes the special place they deserve. It is more than just another filing system, for it is designed to accommodate your truly prized recipes, those which hold a proud place in your cooking repertory and in which you or your family take delight.

Once you complete the entries, the cookbook will be a reflection of your own talents and tastes. After all, how you cook—your ingredients, preparations, serving style, and menus—is as much a part of your

personal character as is the way you dress or wear your hair. Remember, too, that filling in this book can be a continuous hobby. If you don't at present have enough favorite recipes for each category, leave the space blank. In time you will acquire new recipes, and your cookbook will come to measure your growing repertory.

Besides being a convenient reference, your cookbook is a rare gift to your descendants, a precious remembrance of you and your culinary practices. At the same time, you can preserve your own heritage by writing down, wherever appropriate, those recipes you inherited from your relatives. Indeed, the old apprentice system still operates—and not just among the master chefs of the world. You too served a kind of apprenticeship when your mother or some other relative taught you to cook. What you learned will remain part of an oral tradition, easily lost or forgotten, if you don't write it down.

The format of this book offers you the widest possible range of recipe categories. The Special Recipes section at the beginning is for those dishes you use so frequently or that form such a notable part of your cooking treasury that you'd want to find them immediately. Each recipe page, here and throughout the book, has room for ingredients, preparation, and cooking instructions. Following is a blank space for additional information, such as where you got the recipe, what special kinds of cooking utensils should be used, where unusual ingredients can be purchased, and so forth. Don't forget to note down how many people each recipe serves.

You no doubt spend a good deal of time planning the whole menu for a meal, deciding which appetizer and which dessert best set off your main dish and which wine adds that memorable touch. Conceiving a menu course by course is as personal and as creative an effort as preparing a single recipe. The Menus section, therefore, provides a place to list the names of the dishes that make up each meal from breakfast through midnight snacks. In all likelihood, many of the recipes themselves will appear in other sections. By itemizing the individual courses, you can see the entire meal at a glance.

Use the main Recipes section as you did the one for Special Recipes, describing the ingredients and preparation of your favorite dishes. The categories range from "soup to nuts" —from hors d'oeuvres to desserts, condiments, and canning preparations. Whatever your specialties—salads, meats, eggs, breads, desserts—you can find a place for them here.

The Reference section contains handy guides to weights and measures, as well as charts for cooking times, calories, and herbs and spices. There is also space for you to jot down the titles of the cookbooks in your library. Try to add any comments you

have about the usefulness of each book, so that others may benefit from your experience.

Finally, fill in the index at the end. It will enable you to quickly find every recipe in your cookbook. And remember, this is your cookbook, a highly personal portrait of your cuisine, a practical directory of your favorite dishes, and a singular record for future generations.

Special Recipes

Specialties of the House

Recipe Name _____

Ingredients:

Preparation: (Including number of servings)

The Romance of the Recipe

Everyone has special dishes they have perfected over the years, dishes for which they have won renown. Put here the recipes for those marvelous culinary creations that your guests always talk about and remember long after they've gone home.

Specialties of the House

Recipe Name _____

Ingredients:

Preparation: (Including number of servings)

The Romance of the Recipe

15

Specialties of the House

Recipe Name _____

Ingredients:

Preparation: (Including number of servings)

The Romance of the Recipe

Heirloom Recipes

Recipe Name _____

Ingredients:

_____

_____

_____

_____

Preparation: (Including number of servings)

_____

_____

_____

_____

_____

_____

_____

_____

_____

_____

The Romance of the Recipe

_____

_____

Do you still recall the way your grandmother made her special soup? You probably learned this recipe and others like it by word of mouth. Record them here so that you can prepare them often and pass them on to your own children.

Recipe Name _____

Ingredients: _____

_____

_____

Preparation: (Including number of servings)

_____

_____

_____

_____

_____

_____

The Romance of the Recipe

_____

_____

Heirloom Recipes

Recipe Name _____

Ingredients:

Preparation: (Including number of servings)

The Romance of the Recipe

Recipe Name _____

Ingredients:

Preparation: (Including number of servings)

The Romance of the Recipe

Fast Main Dish Recipes

Recipe Name _____

Ingredients:

_____

_____

_____

Preparation: (Including number of servings)

_____

_____

_____

_____

_____

_____

_____

_____

_____

_____

The Romance of the Recipe

_____

Of course, there are days when you don't have time to make that elaborate dish so pleasing to your family. But for these hurried moments you've no doubt learned how to prepare easy, tasty meals they also look forward to eating. Although these dishes may be simple, you still need recipes, which you will find quickly if you enter them here.

Recipe Name _____

Ingredients:

Preparation: (Including number of servings)

The Romance of the Recipe

Fast Main Dish Recipes

Recipe Name _____

Ingredients: _____

_____

_____

_____

Preparation: (Including number of servings)

_____

_____

_____

_____

_____

_____

_____

_____

_____

_____

_____

The Romance of the Recipe

_____

_____

Recipe Name _____

Ingredients:

Preparation: (Including number of servings) _____

The Romance of the Recipe _____

Children's Favorite Recipes

Recipe Name _____

Ingredients:

Preparation: (Including number of servings)

The Romance of the Recipe

What are the dishes your children never tire of eating no matter how often you serve them, those dishes that make their eyes light up when you put the food on the table? Write these recipes and perhaps your children will someday cook them for their own families.

Recipe Name _____

Ingredients: _____

Preparation: (Including number of servings)

The Romance of the Recipe

Children's Favorite Recipes

Recipe Name _____

Ingredients: _____

Preparation: (Including number of servings) _____

The Romance of the Recipe

Recipe Name _____

Ingredients:

Preparation: (Including number of servings)

The Romance of the Recipe

Menus

Breakfast

You surely like to start off the day with a nutritious breakfast. It may be a very simple menu of juice, eggs, bacon, and toast, or some more elaborate assortment of dishes for the times when company is at your table. So include here the satisfying breakfast menus you have worked out over the years.

Brunch

Brunch is that week-end meal which sometimes replaces breakfast and lunch. Because you often serve it to guests, some of the dishes may be unusual. Perhaps you offer eggs benedict instead of scrambled. What are your favorite dishes for a brunch menu?

Lunch

You probably don't have special lunch menus for just you or the family. But your mid-day menus for guests transform a simple lunch into a luncheon. Cold platters, soups, breads—all have a place here.

Coffee or Tea Break

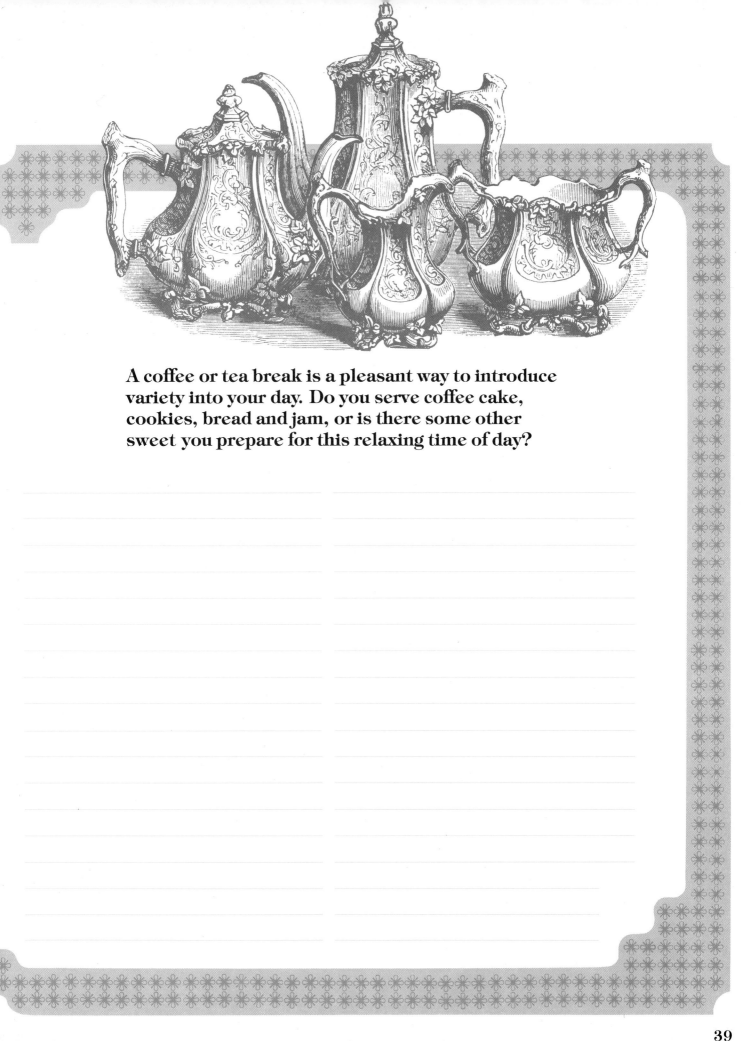

A coffee or tea break is a pleasant way to introduce
variety into your day. Do you serve coffee cake,
cookies, bread and jam, or is there some other
sweet you prepare for this relaxing time of day?

Dinner

Since dinner is for most of us the main meal of the day, we usually give it extra thought. There are more courses to prepare and coordinate, whether you are serving just the family or guests as well. Listing these dishes here will help you remember each dinner menu and assure that future meals you serve are varied and exciting.

Snacks

Munch a morsel,
munch a tidbit,
munch a snackerel.
Afterschool snacks,
TV snacks, midnight snacks,
pet snacks, what is your
favorite munching fare?

Parties

How do you entertain a group
of people? You may offer canapés,
hot and cold hors d'oeuvres,
platters of meat and cheese, or
a whole meal served buffet style.
Whatever your menus for each
occasion, you will want to write
them in here and have them
available for the next party.

Barbecues & Picnics

Outdoor meals are always fun. And you have to think about barbecues and picnics in a different way since you assemble or cook them outside the kitchen. What dishes do you bring together for these informal, happy times?

Special Occasions

This is the place to record your favorite menus for special occasions. What kind of meals do you plan in order to celebrate birthdays, anniversaries, religious holidays, graduations, or those wonderful family get-togethers? These meals will be long remembered and if you list them here, your children may one day carry on the tradition.

Holiday Specialties

Record on these pages those holiday recipes that play a special role in your cuisine—those unusual dishes which enhance the holiday seasons.

A treasured recipe inherited from a loved one, that gourmet preparation which truly marks your skill as a cook.

Holiday Specialties

Memorable Meals I Have Served

Sometimes the dishes you prepare
for a particular meal work so well
together that the meal becomes
a memorable event. Before
you forget that winning combination,
jot it down here. You may also want
to record the names of the guests
who enjoyed your cuisine.

Memorable Meals I Have Served

Recipes

Hors d'oeuvres

Recipe Name _____

Ingredients:

Preparation: (Including number of servings)

The Romance of the Recipe

Recipe Name _____

Ingredients: _____

Preparation: (Including number of servings) _____

The Romance of the Recipe _____

What do you serve your dinner guests before they come to the table? Whether hot or cold, you probably have some favorite hors d'oeuvres with which to welcome your guests when they come in the door.

Hors d'oeuvres

Recipe Name _____

Ingredients: _____

Preparation: (Including number of servings)

The Romance of the Recipe

Recipe Name _____

Ingredients: _____   _____

_____   _____

_____   _____

_____   _____

Preparation: (Including number of servings) _____

The Romance of the Recipe _____

Appetizers

Recipe Name _____

Ingredients: _____

Preparation: (Including number of servings) _____

The Romance of the Recipe _____

Your soups may be light and refreshing treats or hearty bowlfuls that constitute a whole meal. Perhaps you make a soup so popular that your family and friends even call it by your name. The directions for favorite soups are vital additions to your own book of recipes.

Recipe Name _____

Ingredients:

Preparation: (Including number of servings)

The Romance of the Recipe

Soups

Recipe Name _____

Ingredients:

Preparation: (Including number of servings)

The Romance of the Recipe

Recipe Name _____

Ingredients:

Preparation: (Including number of servings)

The Romance of the Recipe

69

Salads and Salad Dressings

Recipe Name _____

Ingredients:

Preparation: (Including number of servings)

The Romance of the Recipe

A meal is not complete without a salad, and a salad is not complete without a dressing. What greens do you use for your favorite salads and with what dressings do you accent them? And what about the wonderful salad you serve as an easy, hot-weather meal in itself?

Recipe Name _____

Ingredients:

Preparation: (Including number of servings)

The Romance of the Recipe

Salads and Salad Dressings

Recipe Name _____

Ingredients:

Preparation: (Including number of servings)

The Romance of the Recipe

Recipe Name _____

Ingredients:

Preparation: (Including number of servings)

The Romance of the Recipe

Vegetables

Recipe Name _____

Ingredients:

Preparation: (Including number of servings)

The Romance of the Recipe

Recipe Name _____

Ingredients:

Preparation: (Including number of servings)

The Romance of the Recipe

Include here your most successful
recipes for vegetables. Are they
sautéd, fried, boiled, steamed, or
served with a sauce? An experienced
cook knows that vegetables, when
well-prepared, enliven a basic meal.

Vegetables

Recipe Name _____

Ingredients:

Preparation: (Including number of servings)

The Romance of the Recipe

Recipe Name _____

Ingredients:

Preparation: (Including number of servings)

The Romance of the Recipe

Meats

Recipe Name _____

Ingredients:

Preparation: (Including number of servings)

The Romance of the Recipe

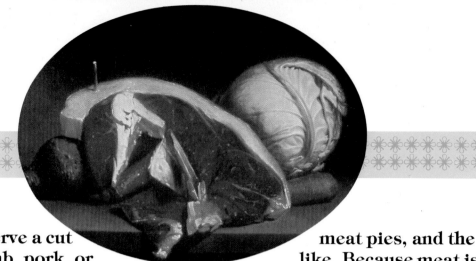

You may serve a cut of beef, lamb, pork, or veal by itself as a simple chop or roast. And you may mix it with other ingredients to make meat loaves, meat stews, meat balls, meat pies, and the like. Because meat is such a basic part of most of our diets, the variety of possible recipes is almost endless. Choose your favorite ones to enter here.

Recipe Name _____

Ingredients:

Preparation: (Including number of servings)

The Romance of the Recipe

Meats

Recipe Name _____

Ingredients:

Preparation: (Including number of servings)

The Romance of the Recipe

Recipe Name _____

Ingredients:

Preparation: (Including number of servings)

The Romance of the Recipe

Meats

Recipe Name _____

Ingredients:

Preparation: (Including number of servings)

The Romance of the Recipe

Recipe Name _____

Ingredients:

Preparation: (Including number of servings)

The Romance of the Recipe

Meats

Recipe Name _____

Ingredients:

_____

_____

_____

_____

Preparation: (Including number of servings)

The Romance of the Recipe

Recipe Name _____

Ingredients:

Preparation: (Including number of servings) _____

The Romance of the Recipe

Poultry

Recipe Name _____

Ingredients:

Preparation: (Including number of servings)

The Romance of the Recipe

Every cook needs recipes for poultry. Poultry is such a versatile food that it can be the main course of both budget meals and gourmet dishes. And whether chicken, duck, turkey, or goose, it is poultry that often becomes the traditional dish for holidays and celebrations. So put down those most important recipes for poultry, plain and fancy.

Recipe Name _____

Ingredients:

Preparation: (Including number of servings)

The Romance of the Recipe

Poultry

Recipe Name _____

Ingredients:

Preparation: (Including number of servings)

The Romance of the Recipe

Recipe Name _____

Ingredients:

Preparation: (Including number of servings)

The Romance of the Recipe

Fish

Recipe Name _____

Ingredients:

Preparation: (Including number of servings)

The Romance of the Recipe

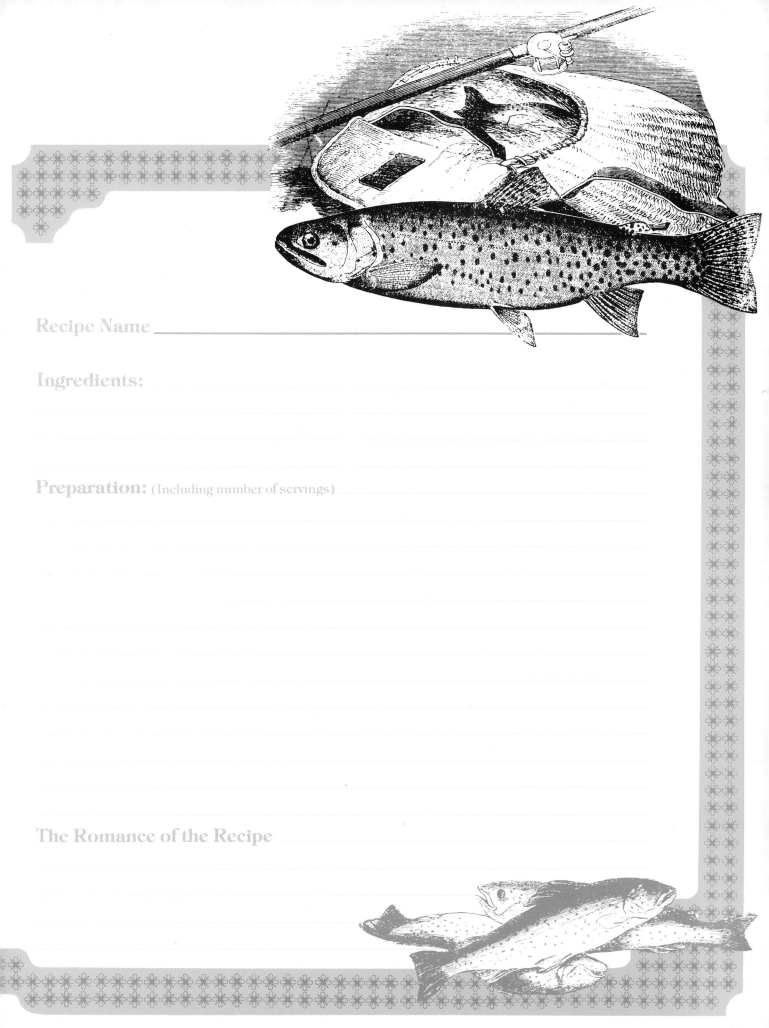

Recipe Name

Ingredients:

Preparation: (Including number of servings)

The Romance of the Recipe

Fish

Recipe Name _____

Ingredients:

Preparation: (Including number of servings)

The Romance of the Recipe

Where you live determines the kind of fish available for cooking. You no doubt have perfected recipes that make the best use of the fish in your region and you can write in your favorite ones here. You may also want to include those recipes for which you cannot get the ingredients but would like to remember for the future.

Recipe Name _____

Ingredients:

Preparation: (Including number of servings)

The Romance of the Recipe

93

Casseroles

Recipe Name _____

Ingredients:

Preparation: (Including number of servings)

The Romance of the Recipe

Recipe Name _____

Ingredients:

Preparation: (Including number of servings)

The Romance of the Recipe

Casseroles are the good cook's mainstay. They are an economical way of using leftovers, stretching expensive ingredients, or incorporating vegetables into the meal. Your family and friends welcome your carefully prepared casseroles and you will want to record the best recipes here.

Sauces and Gravies

Recipe Name _____

Ingredients:

Preparation: (Including number of servings)

The Romance of the Recipe

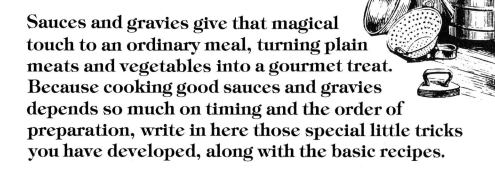

Sauces and gravies give that magical touch to an ordinary meal, turning plain meats and vegetables into a gourmet treat. Because cooking good sauces and gravies depends so much on timing and the order of preparation, write in here those special little tricks you have developed, along with the basic recipes.

Recipe Name _____

Ingredients:

Preparation: (Including number of servings)

The Romance of the Recipe

Egg Dishes and Soufflés

Recipe Name _____

Ingredients:

Preparation: (Including number of servings)

The Romance of the Recipe

Recipe Name _____

Ingredients:

_____

_____

_____

Preparation: (Including number of servings) _____

_____

_____

_____

_____

The Romance of the Recipe

Like chicken, you surely use eggs for a wide variety of meals. Have you any special recipes for omelettes or scrambled eggs? And remember that eggs also are the essential ingredient in soufflés—the most regal of all egg dishes.

Egg Dishes and Soufflés

Recipe Name _____

Ingredients:

Preparation: (Including number of servings)

The Romance of the Recipe

Recipe Name _____

Ingredients:

Preparation: (Including number of servings)

The Romance of the Recipe

Breads and Rolls

Recipe Name _____

Ingredients: _____

Preparation: (Including number of servings) _____

The Romance of the Recipe

Despite the abundance of packaged breads, many cooks still prefer to bake their own. Nothing can replace that tantalizing warm aroma of freshly rising bread. Where did your favorite bread recipes come from? Which ones do you use when you bake bread to give as a friendly gift?

Breads and Rolls

Recipe Name _____

Ingredients:

Preparation: (Including number of servings)

The Romance of the Recipe

Desserts &

Beverages

Desserts

Recipe Name _____

Ingredients:

Preparation: (Including number of servings)

The Romance of the Recipe

Desserts come in many forms. Depending upon the meal and the guests at table, you may serve anything from small tea cookies to rich layer cakes or fancy pies. Perhaps you find fruit compotes, ice creams, and sherberts especially refreshing. So pull out those recipes from your bag of tricks and write them in on these pages.

Recipe Name _____

Ingredients:

Preparation: (Including number of servings)

The Romance of the Recipe

Desserts

Recipe Name _____

Ingredients:

Preparation: (Including number of servings)

The Romance of the Recipe

Recipe Name _____

Ingredients:

_____

_____

_____

Preparation: (Including number of servings) _____

_____

_____

_____

_____

_____

_____

_____

_____

_____

_____

The Romance of the Recipe _____

Desserts

Recipe Name _____

Ingredients:

Preparation: (Including number of servings)

The Romance of the Recipe

Recipe Name _____

Ingredients:

Preparation: (Including number of servings)

The Romance of the Recipe

Favorite Wines

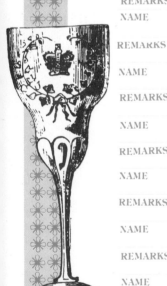

NAME   YEAR

REMARKS

NAME   YEAR

REMARKS

NAME   YEAR

REMARKS

NAME   YEAR

REMARKS

NAME   YEAR

REMARKS

NAME   YEAR

REMARKS

NAME   YEAR

REMARKS

NAME   YEAR

REMARKS

NAME   YEAR

REMARKS

NAME   YEAR

REMARKS

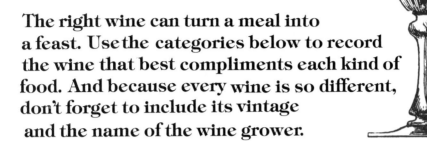

The right wine can turn a meal into a feast. Use the categories below to record the wine that best compliments each kind of food. And because every wine is so different, don't forget to include its vintage and the name of the wine grower.

NAME   YEAR

REMARKS

NAME   YEAR

REMARKS

NAME   YEAR

REMARKS

NAME   YEAR

REMARKS

NAME   YEAR

REMARKS

NAME   YEAR

REMARKS

NAME   YEAR

REMARKS

NAME   YEAR

REMARKS

Beverages

Recipe Name _____

Ingredients:

Preparation: (Including number of servings)

The Romance of the Recipe

Some of the beverages you serve with meals or at a party
—punches, egg nogs, cocktails, milk drinks, and even coffees
or teas—may require mixing or other preparation. Use this
space to write in your favorite beverage recipes, particularly
those that have made a hit with your family and friends.

Recipe Name _____

Ingredients:

Preparation: (Including number of servings)

The Romance of the Recipe

Beverages

Recipe Name _____

Ingredients:

Preparation: (Including number of servings)

The Romance of the Recipe

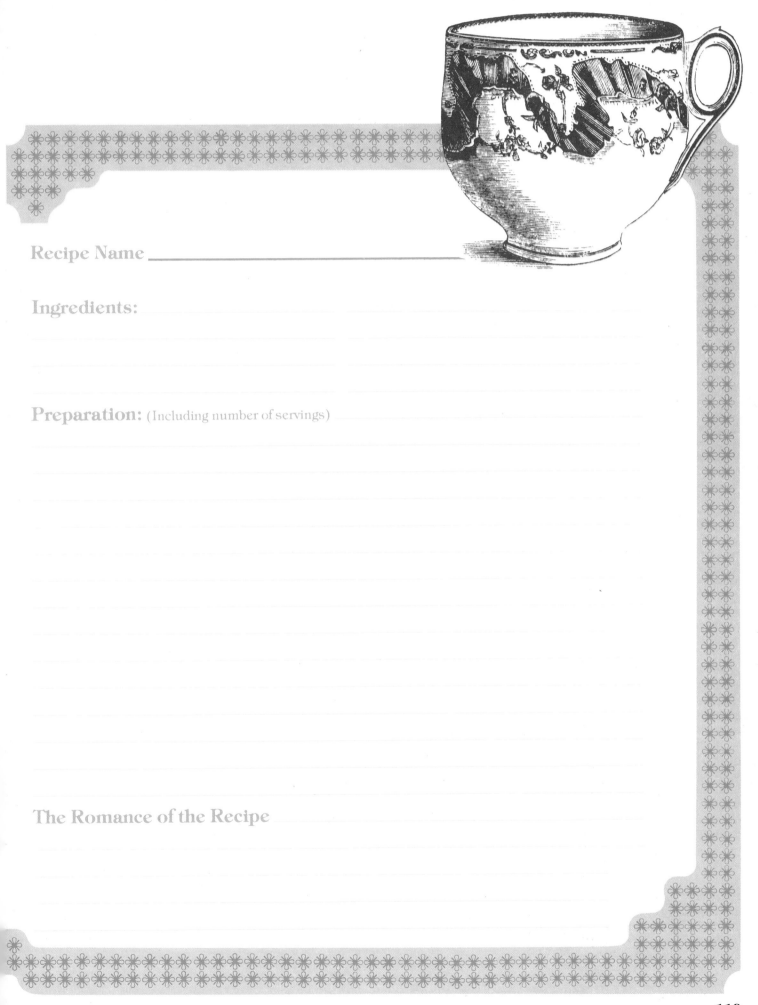

Recipe Name _____

Ingredients:

Preparation: (Including number of servings)

The Romance of the Recipe

Favorite Cheeses

Favorite Cheeses

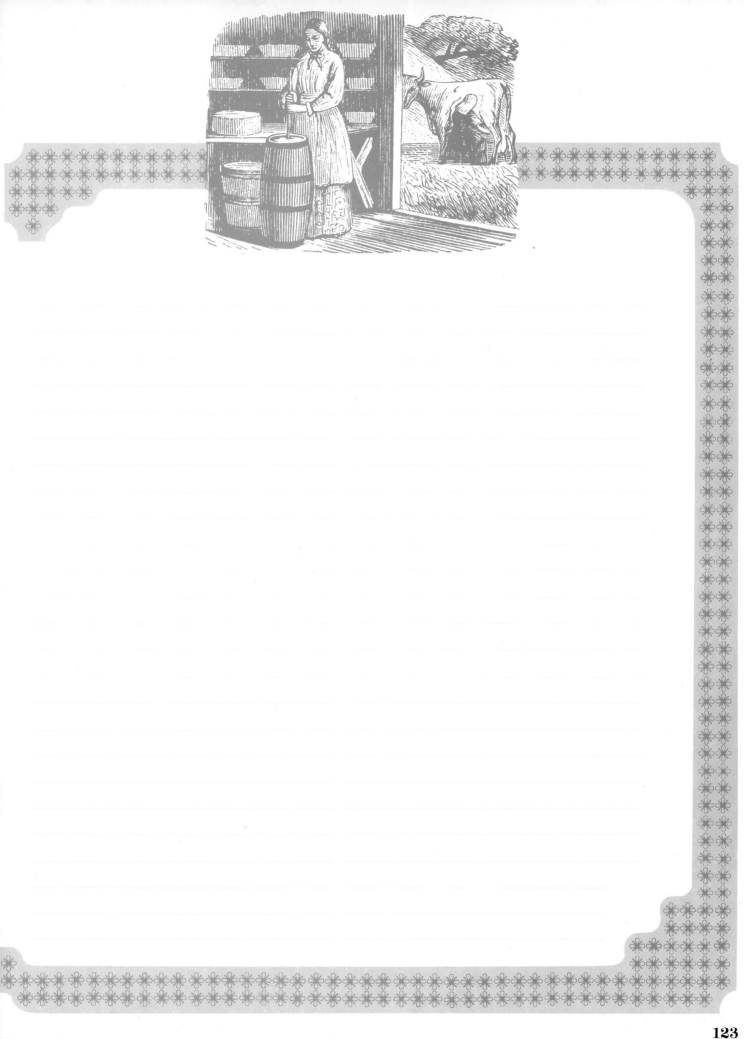

Preserves and Condiments

Recipe Name _____

Ingredients:

Preparation: (Including number of servings)

The Romance of the Recipe

The recipes for these little accents to a meal are often passed down through the generations. This may be why they often accompany the main dishes of traditional or holiday meals. Whether you use the recipes for special occasions or to spark up everyday fare, note your favorite ones here.

Recipe Name _____

Ingredients:

Preparation: (Including number of servings)

The Romance of the Recipe

Preserves and Condiments

Recipe Name _____

Ingredients: _____

Preparation: (Including number of servings) _____

The Romance of the Recipe _____

Recipe Name _____

Ingredients:

Preparation: (Including number of servings)

The Romance of the Recipe

Reference

Herbs and Spices

HERBS	USED IN
Anise	cookies, cakes, breads
Basil	tomatoes, fish, eggs, spaghetti sauce
Bay	stock, soup, stew, stuffing, marinade
Chervil	salad, eggs, soup, veal, chicken
Chives	eggs, salad, potatoes, cream cheese
Coriander	Caribbean and Mexican dishes
Cumin	chili, enchilada, curry, beans, rice
Dill	fish, potatoes, salad, cucumber
Horse-radish	cocktail sauce, boiled meat, fish sauces
Marjoram, sweet and wild	Spanish and Mexican dishes, lamb, mushrooms, sausage, soup, salad
Mint	iced tea, fruit, peas, lamb, jelly, juleps
Mustard	sauces, salad dressing, pickles, cold meats,
Parsley	salad, meats, soup, stew
Rosemary	lamb, poultry, sauces, potatoes, spinach
Saffron	paella, bouillabaisse, rice
Sage	stuffing, pork, goose, herb bread
Savory	poultry, salad, peas, string beans, horse-radish sauce, pork
Sorrel	soup, sauces
Tarragon	salad, chicken, soup, fish, vinegar, sauces
Thyme	tomatoes, lamb, veal, pork, stock
Fines Herbes	A combination of chopped herbs, usually parsley, basil, chives and chervil, added to omelets, sauces, cream soups
Bouquet Garni	a combination of herbs tied together in a cheesecloth bag and put in soups, stews and ragouts. Typically, 3 sprigs parsley, 2 sprigs thyme, white part of 1 leek, 1 celery stalk

(1/3 to 1/2 teaspoon dried = 1 tablespoon fresh)

SPICES	USED IN
Allspice	pickles, relishes, cakes, cookies, pot roast, stew, meatloaf
Cardamom	marinade, mulled wine, coffee, bread, cake, Swedish meatballs
Cloves	ham, mulled wine, tea, fruit, chutney, pickles, boiled meats, soup
Curry Powder	curry, eggs, marinade, sauce
Ginger	cookies, cakes, puddings, pot roast, fruit, sweet potatoes, squash, carrots
Nutmeg	eggnog, spice cake, compote, applesauce, meatloaf, spinach
Pepper	WHITE with sausages, pale-colored foods and sauces; BLACK with dark sauces, red meats, salads; CAYENNE in some sauces, used sparingly

Calorie Counter

A

Abalone, canned, 4 oz.	93
Acerola juice, fresh, 8-oz. glass	58
Alcoholic beverages, see separate listing	
Almonds:	
dried, shelled, ¼ lb.	678
dried, shelled, ½ cup	425
dried, unshelled, ¼ lb.	346
roasted and salted, ¼ lb.	711
roasted and salted, ½ cup	477
roasted and salted, chopped, 1T	37
Apple Butter, 1T	35
Anchovies, canned, 5 fillets	37
Apple juice, canned or bottled, 8-oz. glass	117
Apples:	
fresh, ½ lb.	121
fresh, peeled, 1 average, 2½″ diameter	66
fresh, unpeeled, 1 average, 2½″ diameter	80
baked, with 2T brown sugar, 1 average	184
dried, ¼ lb.	312
Applesauce, canned, sweetened, ½ cup	116
Applesauce, canned, unsweetened, ½ cup	49
Apricot nectar, canned or bottled, 8-oz. glass	143
Apricots:	
fresh, ½ lb.	109
candied, 1 oz.	95
canned, heavy syrup, ½ cup with liquid	111
canned, juice pack, ½ cup with liquid	54
canned, water pack, ½ cup with liquid	38
dried, ¼ lb.	295
dried, cooked, sweetened, ½ cup with liquid	198
dried, cooked, unsweetened, ½ cup with liquid	121
frozen, sweetened, ½ cup	128
Artichokes, French, boiled, drained, 1 average	53
Asparagus:	
raw, spears, ½ lb.	33
boiled, drained, 6 spears	21
boiled, drained, cut spears, ½ cup	18
canned, green, 6 spears	20
canned, white, 6 spears	20
frozen, 6 spears	23
frozen, cuts and tips, ½ cups	20
Avocados:	
California, ½ average	185
California, cubes, ½ cup	130
Florida, ½ average	157
Florida, cubes, ½ cup	98

B

Bacon, broiled or fried, drained, 2 slices	98
Bacon, Canadian, broiled or fried, drained, 1 slice	58
Bamboo shoots, raw, ½ cup	20
Bananas:	
fresh, ½ lb.	131
fresh, 1 average, 6¾″ long	87
fresh, slices, ½ cup	64
Barley, pearled, light, dry, 2T	98
Barley, pearled, Scotch, dry, 2T	87
Bass:	
sea, raw, 4 oz.	106
smallmouth and largemouth, raw, 4 oz.	118
striped, raw, 4 oz.	120
white, raw, 4 oz.	112
Bean, curd, soy, 1 cake, 2½″ x 2½″ x 1″	72
Bean sprouts, mung, raw, ½ cup	16
Bean sprouts, soy, raw, ½ cup	25
Beans, baked:	
with pork and molasses sauce, canned, ½ cup	197
with pork and tomato sauce, canned, ½ cup	160
with tomato sauce, canned, ½ cup	157
Beans, green:	
boiled, drained, ½ cup	16
canned, ½ cup with liquid	21
canned, drained, ½ cup	15
frozen, cut, ½ cup	22
frozen, whole (Birds Eye), ½ cup	23
frozen, French style, ½ cup	23
frozen, with butter sauce, ½ cup	63
Beans, lima:	
boiled, drained, ½ cup	89
canned, ½ cup with liquid	82
canned, drained, ½ cup	77
frozen, baby, ½ cup	114
frozen, Fordhook, ½ cup	96
Beans, pinto, calico, red Mexican, dry, ½ cup	349
Beans, wax:	
boiled, drained, ½ cup	16
canned, ½ cup with liquid	23
canned, drained, ½ cup	18
frozen, cut, ½ cup	25
Beef, choice grade cuts:	
brisket, lean and fat, braised, 4 oz.	470
brisket, lean only, braised, 4 oz.	253
chuck, arm, lean and fat, pot-roasted, 4 oz.	329

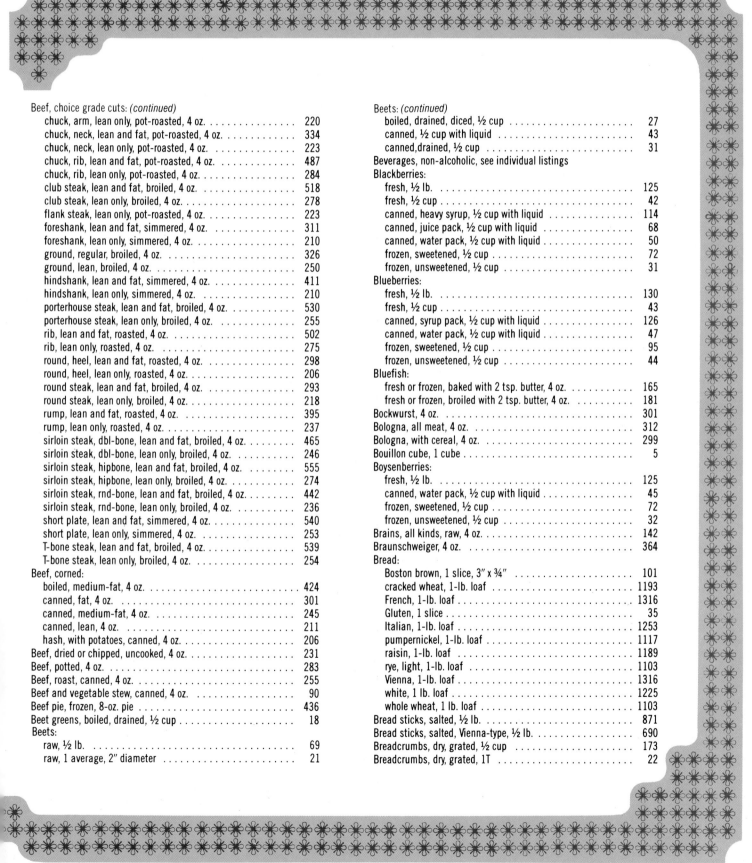

Beef, choice grade cuts: *(continued)*
  chuck, arm, lean only, pot-roasted, 4 oz. 220
  chuck, neck, lean and fat, pot-roasted, 4 oz. 334
  chuck, neck, lean only, pot-roasted, 4 oz. 223
  chuck, rib, lean and fat, pot-roasted, 4 oz. 487
  chuck, rib, lean only, pot-roasted, 4 oz. 284
  club steak, lean and fat, broiled, 4 oz. 518
  club steak, lean only, broiled, 4 oz. 278
  flank steak, lean only, pot-roasted, 4 oz. 223
  foreshank, lean and fat, simmered, 4 oz. 311
  foreshank, lean only, simmered, 4 oz. 210
  ground, regular, broiled, 4 oz. 326
  ground, lean, broiled, 4 oz. 250
  hindshank, lean and fat, simmered, 4 oz. 411
  hindshank, lean only, simmered, 4 oz. 210
  porterhouse steak, lean and fat, broiled, 4 oz. 530
  porterhouse steak, lean only, broiled, 4 oz. 255
  rib, lean and fat, roasted, 4 oz. 502
  rib, lean only, roasted, 4 oz. 275
  round, heel, lean and fat, roasted, 4 oz. 298
  round, heel, lean only, roasted, 4 oz. 206
  round steak, lean and fat, broiled, 4 oz. 293
  round steak, lean only, broiled, 4 oz. 218
  rump, lean and fat, roasted, 4 oz. 395
  rump, lean only, roasted, 4 oz. 237
  sirloin steak, dbl-bone, lean and fat, broiled, 4 oz. 465
  sirloin steak, dbl-bone, lean only, broiled, 4 oz. 246
  sirloin steak, hipbone, lean and fat, broiled, 4 oz. 555
  sirloin steak, hipbone, lean only, broiled, 4 oz. 274
  sirloin steak, rnd-bone, lean and fat, broiled, 4 oz. 442
  sirloin steak, rnd-bone, lean only, broiled, 4 oz. 236
  short plate, lean and fat, simmered, 4 oz. 540
  short plate, lean only, simmered, 4 oz. 253
  T-bone steak, lean and fat, broiled, 4 oz. 539
  T-bone steak, lean only, broiled, 4 oz. 254
Beef, corned:
  boiled, medium-fat, 4 oz. 424
  canned, fat, 4 oz. 301
  canned, medium-fat, 4 oz. 245
  canned, lean, 4 oz. 211
  hash, with potatoes, canned, 4 oz. 206
Beef, dried or chipped, uncooked, 4 oz. 231
Beef, potted, 4 oz. 283
Beef, roast, canned, 4 oz. 255
Beef and vegetable stew, canned, 4 oz. 90
Beef pie, frozen, 8-oz. pie 436
Beet greens, boiled, drained, ½ cup 18
Beets:
  raw, ½ lb. 69
  raw, 1 average, 2″ diameter 21

Beets: *(continued)*
  boiled, drained, diced, ½ cup 27
  canned, ½ cup with liquid 43
  canned, drained, ½ cup 31
Beverages, non-alcoholic, see individual listings
Blackberries:
  fresh, ½ lb. 125
  fresh, ½ cup 42
  canned, heavy syrup, ½ cup with liquid 114
  canned, juice pack, ½ cup with liquid 68
  canned, water pack, ½ cup with liquid 50
  frozen, sweetened, ½ cup 72
  frozen, unsweetened, ½ cup 31
Blueberries:
  fresh, ½ lb. 130
  fresh, ½ cup 43
  canned, syrup pack, ½ cup with liquid 126
  canned, water pack, ½ cup with liquid 47
  frozen, sweetened, ½ cup 95
  frozen, unsweetened, ½ cup 44
Bluefish:
  fresh or frozen, baked with 2 tsp. butter, 4 oz. 165
  fresh or frozen, broiled with 2 tsp. butter, 4 oz. 181
Bockwurst, 4 oz. 301
Bologna, all meat, 4 oz. 312
Bologna, with cereal, 4 oz. 299
Bouillon cube, 1 cube 5
Boysenberries:
  fresh, ½ lb. 125
  canned, water pack, ½ cup with liquid 45
  frozen, sweetened, ½ cup 72
  frozen, unsweetened, ½ cup 32
Brains, all kinds, raw, 4 oz. 142
Braunschweiger, 4 oz. 364
Bread:
  Boston brown, 1 slice, 3″ x ¾″ 101
  cracked wheat, 1-lb. loaf 1193
  French, 1-lb. loaf 1316
  Gluten, 1 slice 35
  Italian, 1-lb. loaf 1253
  pumpernickel, 1-lb. loaf 1117
  raisin, 1-lb. loaf 1189
  rye, light, 1-lb. loaf 1103
  Vienna, 1-lb. loaf 1316
  white, 1 lb. loaf 1225
  whole wheat, 1 lb. loaf 1103
Bread sticks, salted, ½ lb. 871
Bread sticks, salted, Vienna-type, ½ lb. 690
Breadcrumbs, dry, grated, ½ cup 173
Breadcrumbs, dry, grated, 1T 22

Breadfruit, fresh, ½ lb.	180
Broccoli:	
raw, ½ lb.	56
raw, 1 large spear	32
boiled, drained, cut spears, ½ cup	20
frozen, chopped, ½ cup	27
frozen, spears, 1 spear	26
frozen, with butter sauce, ½ cup	60
Brussels sprouts:	
raw, ½ lb.	94
boiled, drained, ½ cup	23
frozen, ½ cup	34
Butter:	
salted or unsalted, 1 cup or ½ lb.	1625
salted or unsalted, 1T	100
salted or unsalted, 1 pat, 16 per ¼ lb.	50
Butterfish, gulf, raw, 4 oz.	108
Butterfish, northern, raw, 4 oz.	192

C

Cabbage:	
white, raw, ½ lb.	49
white, raw, shredded, ½ cup	12
white, boiled in small amount water, drained, ½ cup	17
white, boiled in large amount water, drained, ½ cup	16
red, raw, ½ lb.	64
red, raw, shredded, ½ cup	16
Savoy, raw, ½ lb.	49
Cabbage, Chinese, raw, ½ lb.	31
Cabbage, Chinese, raw, shredded, ½ cup	7
Cabbage, spoon, raw, ½ lb.	35
Cabbage, spoon, boiled, drained, ½ cup	11
Cantaloupe:	
fresh, ½ lb.	34
fresh, ½ melon, 5″ diameter	58
fresh, diced, ½ cup	36
Capicola, 4 oz.	565
Carp, raw, flesh only, 4 oz.	131
Carrots:	
raw, ½ lb.	78
raw, 1 average, 5½″ x 1″	21
boiled, drained, diced, ½ cup	23
canned, ½ cup with liquid	34
canned, drained, ½ cup	23
Casaba melon, fresh, ½ lb.	31
Catsup, tomato, bottled, 1 oz.	30
Catsup, tomato, bottled, 1T	18
Cauliflower:	
raw, ½ lb.	61
boiled, drained, ½ cup	13
frozen, ½ cup	21
Caviar, granular, 1 oz.	74
Caviar, pressed, 1 oz.	89
Celery:	
raw, ½ lb.	29
raw, 1 outer stalk	6
raw, diced, ½ cup	9
boiled, drained, ½ cup	9
Cervelat, dry, 4 oz.	514
Cervelat, soft, 4 oz.	350
Chard, Swiss, raw, ½ lb.	52
Chard, Swiss, cooked, ½ cup	14

Cheese:	
American, processed, 1 oz.	105
American with brick, processed, 1 oz.	101
American with Muenster, processed, 1 oz.	100
blue or Roquefort type, 1 oz.	103
brick, 1 oz.	105
brick, processed, 1 oz.	102
Camembert, domestic, 1 oz.	84
cheddar or American, 1 oz.	111
cheddar or American, grated, 1T	30
cottage, creamed, ½ cup	120
cottage, creamed, 1 oz.	30
cottage, creamed, 1T	17
cottage, uncreamed, ½ cup	98
cottage, uncreamed, 1 oz.	24
cottage, uncreamed, 1T	14
cream, 1 oz.	105
Gouda, 1 oz.	108
Gruyere, 1 oz.	112
Liederkranz Brand, 1 oz.	86
Limburger, 1 oz.	97
Monterey, 1 oz.	105
Mozzarella, 1 oz.	80
Muenster, 1 oz.	101
Nuworld, 1 oz.	104
Old English, processed, 1 oz.	105
Parmesan, 1 oz.	110
Parmesan, grated	29
pimiento, American, processed, 1 oz.	104
Port DuSalut, 1 oz.	101
Provolone, 1 oz.	99
Romano, 1 oz.	110
Romano, grated	30
Roquefort, 1 oz.	105
Swiss, domestic, 1 oz.	104
Swiss, processed, 1 oz.	95
Cherries:	
sour, fresh, ½ lb.	121
sour, fresh, ½ cup	35
sweet, fresh, ½ lb.	143
sweet, fresh, ½ cup	41
candied, 1 oz.	96
candied, 1 average	17
canned, sour, heavy syrup, ½ cup with liquid	116
canned, sour, water pack, ½ cup with liquid	47
canned, sweet, heavy syrup, ½ cup with liquid	106
canned, sweet, water pack, ½ cup with liquid	53
frozen, sour, sweetened, ½ cup	123
frozen, sour, unsweetened, ½ cup	61
Cherries, maraschino, bottled, 2 oz. with liquid	66
Cherries, maraschino, bottled, 2 average	19
Chervil, raw, 1 oz.	16
Chicken:	
broiled, meat only, 4 oz.	155
roasted, dark meat, 4 oz.	210
roasted, light meat, 4 oz.	207
roasted, meat and skin, 4 oz.	283
stewed, meat only, 4 oz.	237
canned, boned, 4 oz.	226
potted, 4 oz.	283

Chicken gizzards, boiled, drained, 4 oz.	168
Chicken pie, frozen, 8-oz. pie	497
Chickpeas, dry, ½ lb.	817
Chickpeas, dry, ½ cup	360
Chicory, raw, ½ lb.	31
Chicory, raw, 10 inner leaves	5
Chicory greens, raw, ½ lb.	37
Chili, with beans, canned, ½ cup	166
Chili, without beans, canned, ½ cup	256
Chili powder, with added seasonings, 1 oz.	96
Chili powder, with added seasonings, 1T	51
Chili sauce, tomato, bottled, 1T	18
Chives, raw, ½ lb.	64
Chives, raw, chopped, 1T	3
Chocolate, bitter or baking, 1 oz.	143
Chop suey, with meat, canned, 4 oz.	71
Chow mein, chicken, without noodles, canned, 4 oz.	43
Chub, raw, flesh only, 4 oz.	165
Citron, candied, 1 oz.	88
Clams:	
hard or round, raw, meat only, 4 oz.	91
soft, raw, meat only, 4 oz.	93
canned, 4 oz. with liquid	59
canned, drained, 4 oz.	112
Cocoa, prepared, 1 cup, ¾ milk, ¼ water	167
Coconut:	
fresh, 1 piece, 2″ x 2½″	156
fresh, shredded, ½ cup	170
dried, unsweetened, ½ lb.	751
dried, sweetened, shredded, ¼ lb.	622
dried, sweetened, shredded, ½ cup	170
Coconut milk (liquid from coconut), ½ cup	27
Cod:	
broiled with butter, 4 oz.	194
canned, 4 oz.	97
dehydrated, lightly salted, 4 oz.	426
dried, salted, 4 oz.	148
Coffee, prepared, plain, 1 cup	2
Collards:	
raw, ½ lb.	70
boiled in small amount water, drained, ½ cup	33
boiled in large amount water, drained, ½ cup	31
frozen, greens (Birds Eye), ½ cup	44
Corn:	
boiled, drained, on cob, 1 ear, 5″ x 1¾″	71
boiled, drained, kernels, ½ cup	69
canned, cream style, ½ cup	94
canned, whole kernels, drained, ½ cup	70
frozen, kernels, ½ cup	77
frozen, with butter sauce, ½ cup	100
Corn, grits, cooked, ½ cup	62
Cornmeal:	
whole grain, unbolted, dry, ½ cup	212
degermed, dry, ½ cup	264
degermed, cooked, ½ cup	60
Cornstarch, 1T	29
Cowpeas, boiled, drained, ½ cup	86
Cowpeas, canned, ½ cup with liquid	70

Crab:	
fresh, steamed, meat only, 4 oz.	105
canned, drained, 4 oz.	115
canned, drained, ½ cup	86
Crabapples, fresh, ½ lb.	142
Cracker crumbs, graham, ½ cup	214
Cracker meal, ½ cup	281
Cracker meal, 1T	44
Cranberries, fresh, ½ lb.	100
Cranberry juice cocktail, canned, 8-oz. glass	163
Cranberry relish with orange, uncooked, ½ cup	250
Cream:	
light or table, ½ cup	253
light or table, 1T	32
half and half, ½ cup	162
half and half, 1T	20
whipping, light, ½ cup unwhipped	358
whipping, light, 1T unwhipped	45
whipping, heavy, ½ cup unwhipped	419
Cucumber:	
fresh, ½ lb.	33
peeled, 1 average, 7½″ x 2″	29
peeled, 6 slices, 2″ x ⅛″	7
Currants:	
black, fresh, ½ lb.	120
red or white, fresh, ½ lb.	110
red or white, fresh, ½ cup	34

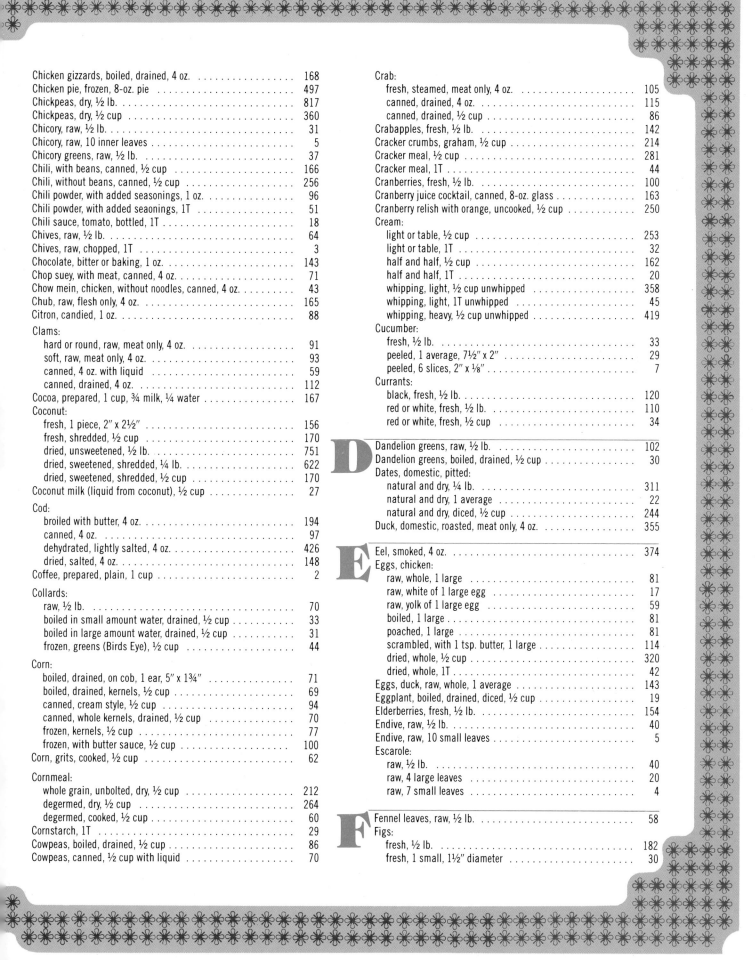

D Dandelion greens, raw, ½ lb.	102
Dandelion greens, boiled, drained, ½ cup	30
Dates, domestic, pitted:	
natural and dry, ¼ lb.	311
natural and dry, 1 average	22
natural and dry, diced, ½ cup	244
Duck, domestic, roasted, meat only, 4 oz.	355

E Eel, smoked, 4 oz.	374
Eggs, chicken:	
raw, whole, 1 large	81
raw, white of 1 large egg	17
raw, yolk of 1 large egg	59
boiled, 1 large	81
poached, 1 large	81
scrambled, with 1 tsp. butter, 1 large	114
dried, whole, ½ cup	320
dried, whole, 1T	42
Eggs, duck, raw, whole, 1 average	143
Eggplant, boiled, drained, diced, ½ cup	19
Elderberries, fresh, ½ lb.	154
Endive, raw, ½ lb.	40
Endive, raw, 10 small leaves	5
Escarole:	
raw, ½ lb.	40
raw, 4 large leaves	20
raw, 7 small leaves	4

F Fennel leaves, raw, ½ lb.	58
Figs:	
fresh, ½ lb.	182
fresh, 1 small, 1½″ diameter	30

Figs: *(continued)*
    candied, 1 oz. 85
    canned, 3 figs with 2T heavy syrup 96
    dried, ¼ lb. 311
    dried, 1 large, 2″ x 1″ 57
Filberts:
    shelled, ¼ lb. 719
    unshelled, ¼ lb. 331
    10-12 nuts 95
Finnan haddie, 4 oz. 117
Fish cakes, fried, frozen, 4 oz. 306
Fish flakes, canned, 4 oz. 126
Flounder, fresh or frozen, baked with 2 tsp. butter, 4 oz. 222
Flour:
    corn, 1 cup sifted 405
    rye, dark, 1 cup sifted 262
    rye, light, 1 cup sifted 286
    wheat, all-purpose, 1 cup sifted 400
    wheat, bread, 1 cup sifted 401
    wheat, cake or pastry, 1 cup sifted 364
Frankfurters:
    cooked, 4 oz. 345
    cooked, 1 average 151
    canned, 4 oz. 251
Fruit cocktail, canned, heavy syrup, ½ cup with liquid 97
Fruit cocktail, canned, water pack, ½ cup with liquid 44

G
Garlic, raw, 1 oz. 39
Garlic, raw, 1 average clove 3
Gelatin, unflavored, dry, 1 envelope 27
Gelatin drink, cranberry or orange, dry, 1 envelope 79
Ginger root, fresh, 1 oz. 14
Ginger root, candied, 1 oz. 96
Goose, roasted, meat only, 4 oz. 266
Goose, roasted, meat and skin, 4 oz. 503
Gooseberries:
    fresh, ½ lb. 88
    fresh, ½ cup 29
    canned, heavy syrup, ½ cup with liquid 108
    canned, water pack, ½ cup with liquid 31
Grape juice, canned or bottled, 8-oz. glass. 168
Grape juice, frozen, sweetened, diluted, 8-oz. glass 131
Grape juice drink, canned or bottled, 8-oz. glass 134
Grapes:
    American type—Concord, Delaware, etc., fresh, ½ lb. 99
    American type—Concord, Delaware, etc., fresh, ½ cup 33
    European type—Thompson seedless, etc., fresh, ½ lb. 135
    European type—Thompson seedless, etc., fresh, ½ cup 48
    canned, water pack, ½ cup with liquid 51
Grapefruit:
    pink, fresh, ½ average, 4½″ diameter 58
    pink, fresh, sections, ½ cup 39
    white, fresh, seeded, ½ average, 4½″ diameter 52
    white, fresh, seedless, ½ average, 4½″ diameter 53
    white, fresh, sections, ½ cup 38
    canned, syrup pack, ½ cup with liquid 87
    canned, water pack, ½ cup with liquid 36
Grapefruit juice:
    fresh, 8-oz. glass 96
    canned, sweetened, 8-oz. glass 133

Grapefruit juice: *(continued)*
    canned, unsweetened, 8-oz. glass 101
    dehydrated, crystals with water, 8-oz. glass 99
    frozen, sweetened, diluted, 8-oz. glass 117
    frozen, unsweetened, diluted, 8-oz. glass 101
Grapefruit-orange juice:
    canned, sweetened, 8-oz. glass 125
    canned, unsweetened, 8-oz. glass 106
    canned, unsweetened, diluted, 8-oz. glass 109
Grapefruit peel, candied, 1 oz. 90
Grapefruit peel, candied, grated, 1T 32
Grouper, raw, flesh only, 4 oz. 99
Guavas:
    fresh, ½ lb. 137
    fresh, 1 small 48
    fresh, strawberry, ½ lb. 145

H
Haddock:
    frozen, fillets (Birds Eye), 2 fillets, 4 oz. 88
    smoked, 4 oz. 117
Halibut:
    fresh or frozen, broiled with 2 tsp. butter, 4 oz. 188
    smoked, 4 oz. 254
Ham:
    boiled, 4 oz. 266
    fresh, medium-fat, roasted, 4 oz. 426
    light-cure, medium-fat, roasted, 4 oz. 329
    light-cure, lean only, roasted, 4 oz. 213
    long-cure, country style, medium-fat, 4 oz. 443
    long-cure, country style, lean only, 4 oz. 353
Headcheese, 4 oz. 305
Heart:
    beef, braised, 4 oz. 214
    calf, braised, 4 oz. 237
    chicken, simmered, 4 oz. 197
Herring:
    raw, Atlantic, 4 oz. 200
    raw, Pacific, 4 oz. 111
    canned, plain, 4 oz. with liquid 236
    canned, in tomato sauce, 4 oz. with liquid 200
    pickled, Bismarck-type, 4 oz. 253
    salted or brined, 4 oz. 247
    smoked, bloaters, 4 oz. 222
    smoked, hard, 4 oz. 340
    smoked, kippered, 4 oz. 239
Honey, strained or extracted, 1 oz. 86
Honey, strained or extracted, 1T 64
Honeydew melon:
    fresh, ½ lb. 47
    fresh, 1 wedge, 2″ x 7″ 49
    fresh, ½ cup diced 40
Horseradish, raw, 1 oz. 18
Horseradish, prepared, 1 oz. 11

J
Jams and preserves, all flavors, 1 oz. 77
Jams and preserves, all flavors, 1T 54
Jellies, all flavors, 1 oz. 78
Jellies, all flavors, 1T 55
Jujube, fresh, ½ lb. 222
Jujube, dried, ½ lb. 580

Junket, powder prepared with whole milk, ½ cup 115
Junket, tablet prepared with whole milk, ½ cup 110

Kale:
    raw, ½ lb. 77
    boiled, drained, ½ cup 15
    frozen, chopped (Birds Eye), ½ cup . . . 29
Kidney, beef, braised, 4 oz. 287
Kingfish, raw, flesh only, 4 oz. 119
Knockwurst, 4 oz. 317
Kohlrabi, raw, without leaves, ½ lb. 48
Kohlrabi, boiled, drained, ½ cup 19
Kumquats, fresh, ½ lb. 137
Kumquats, fresh, 4 average 39

Lamb, choice grade cuts:
    chop, loin, lean and fat, broiled, 4.8 oz. with bone 402
    chop, loin, lean only, broiled, 4.8 oz. with bone 140
    leg, lean and fat, roasted, 4 oz. 318
    leg, lean only, roasted, 4 oz. 212
    shoulder, lean and fat, roasted, 4 oz. 385
    shoulder, lean only, roasted, 4 oz. 234
Lambsquarters, raw, 4 oz. 49
Lambsquarters, boiled, drained, ½ cup 32
Lard:
    ½ lb. 2046
    1 cup 1984
    1T 122
Leeks, raw, ½ lb. 62
Leeks, raw, 1 average 17
Lemon juice:
    fresh, ½ cup 30
    fresh, 1T 4
    canned or bottled, unsweetened, ½ cup 28
    canned or bottled, unsweetened, 1T 3
Lemons, fresh, ½ lb. 45
Lemons, fresh, 1 average, 2½" diameter 45
Lentils:
    whole, uncooked, ½ cup 374
    whole, uncooked, ½ cup 102
    split, uncooked, ½ cup 379
Lettuce:
    Boston or Bibb, ½ lb. 24
    Boston or Bibb, 1 head, 4" diameter 31
    iceberg, ½ lb. 28
    iceberg, 1 head, 4¾" diameter 59
    iceberg, 3 average leaves 6
    romaine, ½ lb. 26
    romaine, 3 leaves, 8" long 5
    Simpson or looseleaf, ½ lb. 26
    Simpson or looseleaf, 2 large leaves . . . 9
Limes, fresh, ½ lb. 54
Limes, fresh, 1 average, 1½" long 19
Liver:
    beef, fried, 4 oz. 260
    calf, fried, 4 oz. 296
    chicken, simmered, 4 oz. 187
    hog, fried, 4 oz. 275
    lamb, broiled, 4 oz. 298
    turkey, simmered, 4 oz. 197

Liverwurst, fresh, 4 oz. 350
Liverwurst, smoked, 4 oz. 364
Lobster, canned or cooked, meat only, 4 oz. . . 108
Lobster paste, 1 oz. 51
Loganberries, fresh, ½ lb. 134
Loganberries, fresh, ½ cup 45
Loquats, fresh, ½ lb. 84

Macadamia nuts:
    shelled, ¼ lb. 784
    unshelled, ¼ lb. 243
    6 nuts 104
Macaroni:
    boiled 8-10 minutes, drained, ½ cup . . . 96
    boiled 14-20 minutes, drained, ½ cup . . 78
Mackerel:
    fresh or frozen, broiled with 2 tsp. butter, 4 oz. 262
    canned, Atlantic, 4 oz. with liquid 208
    canned, Pacific, 4 oz. with liquid 204
    salted, 4 oz. 346
    smoked, 4 oz. 250
Malt, dry, 1 oz. 104
Mangos, fresh, ½ lb. 101
Mangos, fresh, 1 average, 3¾" long 134
Margarine:
    salted or unsalted, 1 cup or ½ lb. 1633
    salted or unsalted, 1T 102
    salted or unsalted, 1 pat, 16 per ¼ lb. . . 51
Milk, cow's:
    whole, 3.5% fat, 8-oz. glass 159
    whole, 3.7% fat, 8-oz. glass 161
    buttermilk, cultured, 8-oz. glass 89
    skim, 8-oz. glass 89
    dry, whole, 1 cup 517
    dry, whole, 1 oz., 4T 142
    dry, nonfat, instant, 1 cup 251
    dry, nonfat, instant, 1 oz., 4T 102
Milk, goat's, whole, 8-oz. glass 163
Mortadella, 4 oz. 358
Mushrooms, raw, ½ lb. 61
Mushrooms, canned, 4 oz. with liquid 19
Mussels, raw, meat only, 4 oz. 108
Mussels, canned, drained, 4 oz. 130
Mustard greens:
    raw, ½ lb. 49
    boiled, drained, ½ cup 16
    frozen, ½ cup 19
Mustard spinach, raw, ½ lb. 50
Mustard spinach, boiled, drained, ½ cup 14
Mustard, prepared, brown, 1 oz. 26
Mustard, prepared, yellow, 1 oz. 21

Nectarines, fresh, ½ lb. 134
Nectarines, fresh, 1 average 30
Noodles, egg, cooked, ½ cup 100
Noodles, fried, chow mein style, canned, 4 oz. 555

O

Oil:

corn, 1T	121
olive, 1T	125
peanut, 1T	124
safflower, 1T	128
salad or cooking, 1T	124
soybean, 1T	125

Okra:

raw, ½ lb.	70
boiled, drained, 8 pods, 3″ long	25

Olives, pickled, canned or bottled:

green, 4 medium or 3 large	15
ripe, Mission, 3 small or 2 large	15

Onions, mature:

raw, ½ lb.	79
raw, 1 average, 2½″ diameter	40
raw, chopped, 1T	4
boiled, drained, ½ cup	30
dehydrated, flakes, 1 oz.	99

Onions, green:

raw, bulb and entire top, ½ lb.	79
raw, bulb and white part, ½ lb.	38
raw, bulb and white part, 3 small	11

Orange juice:

California, Navel, fresh, 8-oz. glass	120
California, Valencia, fresh, 8-oz. glass	117
Florida, early and midseason, fresh, 8-oz. glass	99
Florida, Valencia, fresh, 8-oz. glass	112
canned, sweetened, 8-oz. glass	129
canned, unsweetened, 8-oz. glass	120
dehydrated, crystals with water, 8-oz. glass	114
frozen, diluted, 8-oz. glass	112

Orange peel, candied, 1 oz.	90
Orange peel, candied, grated, 1T	32

Oranges:

Florida, all varieties, fresh, ½ lb.	79
Florida, all varieties, fresh, 1 average, 3″ diameter	75
Navel, fresh, ½ lb.	79
Navel, fresh, 1 average, 2⅞″ diameter	60
sections, fresh, ½ cup	47

Oysters:

Eastern, raw, meat only, 4 oz.	75
Pacific or Western, raw, meat only, 4 oz.	103
canned, 4 oz. with liquid	86

P

Papaya juice, canned, 8-oz. glass	120
Papayas, fresh, ½ lb.	60
Papayas, fresh, ½″ cubes, ½ cup	36
Parsley, raw, ½ lb.	100
Parsley, raw, chopped, 1T	2
Parsnips, raw, ½ lb.	147
Parsnips, boiled, drained, ½ cup	51
Passionfruit, fresh, ½ lb.	106
Pâté de foie gras, canned, 1 oz.	131
Peach nectar, canned, 8-oz. glass	120

Peaches:

fresh, 1 average, 2″ diameter	35
fresh, sliced, ½ cup	33
candied, 1 oz.	90

Peaches: *(continued)*

canned, heavy syrup, ½ cup with liquid	100
canned, 2 medium halves with 2T heavy syrup	88
canned, water pack, ½ cup with liquid	38
dried, ¼ lb.	297
dried, ½ cup	210
dried, cooked, sweetened, ½ cup with liquid	190
dried, cooked, unsweetened, ½ cup with liquid	111
frozen, sweetened, sliced, ½ cup	110

Peanuts:

raw, shelled, ¼ lb.	640
raw, unshelled, ¼ lb.	467
roasted, shelled, ¼ lb.	660
roasted, unshelled, ¼ lb.	442
roasted and salted, ¼ lb.	664
roasted and salted, ½ cup halves	421
roasted and salted, chopped, 1T	54

Pear nectar, canned, 8-oz. glass	130

Pears:

fresh, ½ lb.	126
fresh, 1 average, 2½″ diameter	100
candied, 1 oz.	86
canned, heavy syrup, ½ cup with liquid	97
canned, 2 medium halves with 2T heavy syrup	89
canned, water pack, ½ cup with liquid	39
dried, ¼ lb.	304
dried, ½ cup	214

Peas, black-eye, canned, ½ cup with liquid	70
Peas, black-eye, frozen (Birds Eye), ½ cup	92

Peas, green:

boiled, drained, ½ cup	57
canned, ½ cup with liquid	82
canned, drained, ½ cup	70
frozen, ½ cup	69
frozen, with butter sauce, ½ cup	97

Peas, split, boiled, drained, ½ cup	115
Peas and carrots, frozen, ½ cup	52

Pecans:

shelled, ¼ lb.	779
unshelled, ¼ lb.	413

Peppers, hot, chili:

green, raw, ½ lb.	62
red, raw, ½ lb.	108
dried, ground, see Chili powder	

Peppers, sweet, green:

raw, ½ lb.	41
raw, seeded, 1 average	14
raw, seeded, diced, ½ cup	10
boiled, drained, seeded, 1 average	11

Perch:

ocean, fresh or frozen, baked with 2 tsp. butter, 4 oz.	160
white, raw, 1 fillet, 4 oz.	134
frozen fillets (Birds Eye), 2 fillets, 4 oz.	100

Persimmons:

Japanese or kaki, seedless, fresh, ½ lb.	147
Japanese or kaki, seedless, fresh, 1 average	81
native, fresh, ½ lb.	236

Pickle relish:

barbecue (Heinz), 1T	32
hamburger (Heinz), 1T	17
sour, 1 oz.	8
sour, 1T	2
sweet, 1 oz.	39
sweet, 1T	18

Pickles, cucumber:

dill, 4 oz.	12
dill, 1 large, 4" x 1¾"	15
fresh, bread-and-butter, 4 oz.	83
fresh, bread-and-butter, 1 average slice	6
sour, 4 oz.	11
sour, 1 large, 4" x 1¾"	14
sweet, 4 oz.	166
sweet, 1 average, 2¾" x ¾"	29

Pickles, chowchow, sour, 4 oz.	33
Pickles, chowchow, sweet, 4 oz.	132
Pigs' feet, pickled, 4 oz.	226

Pike, raw:

blue, flesh only, 4 oz.	102
northern, flesh only, 4 oz.	100
wall-eye, flesh only, 4 oz.	106

Pilinuts, shelled, ¼ lb.	759
Pilinuts, unshelled, ¼ lb.	137
Pimientos, canned, 4 oz. with liquid	31
Pimientos, canned, 1 average	10

Pineapple:

fresh, ½ lb.	62
fresh, 1 slice, 3½" x ¾"	44
fresh, diced, ½ cup	36
candied, 1 oz.	90
canned, heavy syrup, chunks, ½ cup with liquid	85
canned, heavy syrup, crushed, ½ cup with liquid	96
frozen, sweetened, chunks, ½ cup	100

Pineapple juice, canned, unsweetened, 8-oz. glass	137
Pineapple juice, frozen, unsweetened, diluted, 8-oz. glass	129
Pineapple-grapefruit juice drink, canned, 8-oz. glass	134
Pineapple-orange juice drink, canned, 8-oz. glass	134

Plums:

Damson, fresh, ½ lb.	136
Damson, fresh, 1 average, 2" diameter	36
Japanese and hybrid, fresh, ½ lb.	103
prune-type, fresh, ½ lb.	160
prune-type, fresh, 1 average	24
canned, purple, 3 plums with 2T heavy syrup	101

Pomegranates, fresh, ½ lb.	80
Pompano, raw, flesh only, 4 oz.	188

Pork:

Boston butt, lean and fat, roasted, 4 oz.	404
Boston butt, lean only, roasted, 4 oz.	279
chop, lean and fat, broiled, 3.5 oz. with bone	260
chop, lean only, broiled, 3.5 oz. with bone	130
loin, lean and fat, roasted, 4 oz.	412
loin, lean only, roasted, 4 oz.	290

Potatoes, white:

baked, including skin, 1 small	93
boiled, in skin, 1 small	76
boiled, peeled, 1 small	65

Potatoes, white: (continued)

canned, 4 oz. with liquid	50
canned, 3-4 very small	96
French fried, 10 pieces, 2" long	156
frozen, hash-browned, heated, ½ cup	224
frozen, mashed, heated, ½ cup	93

Potatoes, sweet:

baked, peeled, 1 average, 5" x 2"	155
boiled, peeled, 1 average	123
candied, 1 average	294
canned, vacuum or solid pack, ½ cup	109
yams, boiled, drained, diced, ½ cup	105

Pretzels, 4 oz.	442
Pretzels, sticks, 5 small sticks	20
Prickly pears, fresh, ½ lb.	42
Prune juice, canned or bottled, 8-oz. glass	197

Prunes:

dehydrated, nugget-type, ¼ lb.	390
dried, large-size, ¼ lb.	225
dried, large-size, 1 average	19
dried, medium-size, ¼ lb.	246
dried, medium-size, 1 average	15
dried, small-size, ¼ lb.	237
dried, small-size, 1 average	11
dried, cooked, unsweetened, ½ cup with liquid	137

Pumpkin, fresh, ½ lb.	42
Pumpkin, canned, ½ cup	38
Pumpkin seeds, dry, hulled, ¼ lb.	627

Q

Quail, raw, boned, 4 oz.	172
Quinces, fresh, ¼ lb.	79

R

Rabbit, domestic, meat only, stewed, 4 oz.	246
Radishes, raw, without tops, ½ lb.	35
Radishes, raw, 4 small	7
Radishes, Oriental, raw, ½ lb.	34
Raisins, dried, ¼ lb.	328
Raisins, dried, ½ cup	231

Raspberries:

black, fresh, ½ lb.	161
black, fresh, ½ cup	45
red, fresh, ½ lb.	126
red, fresh, ½ cup	35
canned, black, water pack, ½ cup with liquid	51
canned, red, water pack, ½ cup with liquid	35

Red snapper, raw, flesh only, 4 oz.	105

Rhubarb:

fresh, without leaves, ½ lb.	31
cooked, sweetened, ½ cup	192

Rice:

brown, cooked, ½ cup	100
white, milled, cooked, ½ cup	92
white, parboiled, long grain, cooked, ½ cup	89

Rutabagas, raw, without tops, ½ lb.	89
Rutabagas, boiled, drained, cubes, ½ cup	35

Salad dressings, commercial:

blue cheese, 1T	81
French, 1T	62
Italian, 1T	83
mayonnaise, 1T	108
mayonnaise-type, 1T	65
Roquefort, 1T	81
Russian, 1T	89
Thousand Island, 1T	75

Salami, cooked, 4 oz.	353
Salami, dry, 4 oz.	510

Salmon:

fresh or frozen steak, baked with 2 tsp. butter, 4 oz.	160
fresh or frozen steak, broiled with 2 tsp. butter, 4 oz.	239
canned, Atlantic, 4 oz.	230
canned, chinook, 4 oz.	238
canned, pink, 4 oz.	160
canned, red, 4 oz.	194
smoked, 4 oz.	200

Sandwich spread relish, 1 oz.	107

Sardines:

canned in brine, Pacific, 4 oz. with liquid	222
canned in mustard, Pacific, 4 oz. with liquid	222
canned in oil, Atlantic, drained, 4 oz.	189
canned in tomato sauce, Pacific, 4 oz. with liquid	224

Sauces:

barbecue, 1T	17
hot pepper, 1T	3
soy, 1T	9
tartar, 1T	74
tomato, canned, ½ cup	35
white, medium, ½ cup	215
white, thin, ½ cup	148

Sauerkraut, canned, ½ cup with liquid	21

Sausages, pork:

brown-and-serve, cooked, 4 oz.	479
links or bulk, cooked, 4 oz.	538
links, smoked, country-style, 4 oz.	391
canned, drained, 4 oz.	434
Vienna, canned, drained, 4 oz.	274

Scallops, bay or sea, steamed, 4 oz.	128
Scallops, breaded, fried, frozen, reheated, 4 oz.	220
Scrapple, 4 oz.	244

Shad:

fresh, baked with 2 tsp. butter, 4 oz.	222
fresh, roe, broiled with 2 tsp. butter, 4 oz.	137
canned, 4 oz. with liquid	172

Sesame seeds, decorticated, 1 oz.	165
Sesame seeds, whole, 1 oz.	160
Shallot bulbs, raw, ½ lb.	144
Shortening, 1T	103
Shrimp, canned, 4 oz. with liquid	91
Shrimp, canned, drained, 4 oz.	132
Soybeans, boiled, drained, ½ cup	89

Spaghetti:

boiled 8-10 minutes, drained, ½ cup	96
boiled 14-20 minutes, drained, ½ cup	78
canned, in tomato sauce with cheese, 4 oz.	86
canned, with ground beef (Franco-American), 4 oz.	135

Spaghetti: *(continued)*

canned, with hot dogs (Heinz), 4 oz.	118
canned, with meat balls in tomato sauce, 4 oz.	117

Spinach:

raw, trimmed, packaged, ½ lb.	59
boiled, drained, ½ cup	21
canned, drained, ½ cup	22
frozen, leaf, ½ cup	24
frozen, chopped, ½ cup	23

Squash, summer:

scallop variety, boiled, drained, ½ cup	17
yellow, boiled, drained, ½ cup	16
zucchini, boiled, drained, ½ cup	13
frozen, yellow, ½ cup	21

Squash, winter:

acorn, baked, mashed, ½ cup	57
acorn, boiled, mashed, ½ cup	35
butternut, baked, mashed, ½ cup	70
butternut, boiled, mashed, ½ cup	42
hubbard, baked, mashed, ½ cup	52
hubbard, boiled, mashed, ½ cup	31
frozen, cooked, ½ cup	43

Strawberries:

fresh, ½ lb.	81
fresh, capped, ½ cup	28
canned, water pack, ½ cup with liquid	29
frozen, halves (Birds Eye), ½ cup	155
frozen, whole (Birds Eye), ½ cup	98
frozen, sweetened, sliced, 1-lb. can or carton	294

Sturgeon, smoked, 4 oz.	169
Sturgeon, steamed, 4 oz.	182

Sugar, beet or cane:

brown, firm-packed, 1 cup	821
brown, firm-packed, 1T	52
granulated, 1 cup	770
granulated, 1T	46
lump, 1 piece, 1⅛″ x ¾″ x ⅜″	23
powdered, stirred, 1 cup	493
powdered, stirred, 1T	31

Sunflower seeds, hulled, ¼ lb.	635

Sweetbreads:

beef, braised, 4 oz.	363
calf, braised, 4 oz.	191
lamb, braised, 4 oz.	198

Swordfish:

fresh or frozen steak, broiled with 2 tsp. butter, 4 oz.	194
canned, 4 oz. with liquid	116

Syrups:

chocolate, thin-type, 1T	49
corn, light or dark, 1T	58
maple, 1T	50
molassses, cane, light, 1T	50
molasses, cane, medium, 1T	46
molasses, cane, blackstrap, 1T	43
molasses, cane, Barbados, 1T	54
sorghum, 1T	51

T

Tamarinds, fresh, ½ lb.	260
Tangerine juice:	
fresh, 8-oz. glass	108
canned, sweetened, 8-oz. glass	125
canned, unsweetened, 8-oz. glass	107
frozen, unsweetened, 8-oz. glass	114
Tangerines, fresh, ½ lb.	77
Tangerines, fresh, 1 average, 2½″ diameter	39
Taro, raw, leaves and stems, ½ lb.	91
Taro, raw, tubers, ½ lb.	187
Tea, bags or loose, prepared, plain, 1 cup	1
Tea, instant, prepared, plain, 1 cup	4
Thuringer, 4 oz.	348
Tomato juice, canned or bottled, 8-oz. glass	46
Tomato paste, canned, 4 oz.	93
Tomato puree, canned, 4 oz.	44
Tomatoes:	
fresh, ½ lb.	50
fresh, 1 average, 2½″ diameter	33
boiled, ½ cup	31
canned, ½ cup with liquid	25
canned, stewed (Hunt's), ½ cup	32
Tongue:	
beef, medium-fat, braised, 4 oz.	277
calf, braised, 4 oz.	181
hog, braised, 4 oz.	287
lamb, braised, 4 oz.	288
Tripe, beef, pickled, 4 oz.	70
Trout, rainbow, canned, 4 oz.	237
Tuna, canned:	
in oil, 4 oz. with liquid	327
in oil, drained, 4 oz.	223
in water, 4 oz. with liquid	144
Turkey:	
dark meat, roasted, 4 oz.	230
light meat, roasted, 4 oz.	200
skin only, roasted, 4 oz.	511
giblets, simmered, 4 oz.	264
Turkey, potted, 4 oz.	283

Turnip greens:	
raw, ½ lb.	64
boiled, small amount water, short time, drained, ½ cup	15
boiled, large amount water, long time, drained, ½ cup	14
canned, ½ cup with liquid	21
frozen, ½ cup	22
Turnips, boiled, drained, ½ cup	18

V

Veal:	
chuck, medium-fat, braised, 4 oz.	266
flank, medium-fat, stewed, 4 oz.	442
foreshank, medium-fat, stewed, 4 oz.	245
loin, medium-fat, broiled, 4 oz.	267
plate, medium-fat, stewed, 4 oz.	344
rib, medium-fat, roasted, 4 oz.	305
round with rump, medium-fat, broiled, 4 oz.	245
Vinegar, cider, 1T	2
Vinegar, distilled, 1T	2

W

Water chestnuts, Chinese, raw, ½ lb.	136
Watercress, raw, ¼ lb.	20
Watercress, raw, 5 sprigs	1
Watermelon:	
fresh, ½ lb.	27
fresh, 1 wedge, 4″ x 8″	111
fresh, cubes or balls, ½ cup	26
Weakfish, broiled, 4 oz.	237
Wheat germ, commercial, 1T	29
Whitefish, smoked, 4 oz.	176

Y

Yeast:	
baker's, compressed, 1 oz.	24
baker's dry, active, 1 oz.	80
brewer's, dry, debittered, 1 oz.	80
brewer's, dry, debittered, 1T	23
Yogurt:	
plain, made from partially skimmed milk, 1 cup	123
plain, made from whole milk, 1 cup	153

Favorite Cookbooks

Metric Conversion Charts

WEIGHT CONVERSION FACTORS

TO CONVERT	TO	MULTIPLY BY
ounces	grams	28.35
pounds	kilograms	.45

TO CONVERT	TO	MULTIPLY BY
grams	ounces	.035
kilograms	pounds	2.20

WEIGHT CONVERSION CHARTS

POUNDS & KILOGRAMS.

Pounds to Kilograms	Kilograms to Pounds
1 lb .... .45 kg	1 kg .... 2.20 lb
2 lb .... .91 kg	2 kg .... 4.41 lb
3 lb ....1.36 kg	3 kg .... 6.61 lb
4 lb ....1.81 kg	4 kg .... 8.82 lb
5 lb ....2.27 kg	5 kg ....11.02 lb
6 lb ....2.72 kg	6 kg ....13.23 lb
7 lb ....3.18 kg	7 kg ....15.43 lb
8 lb ....3.63 kg	8 kg ....17.64 lb
9 lb ....4.08 kg	9 kg ....19.84 lb
10 lb ....4.54 kg	10 kg ....22.05 lb

AVOIRDUPOIS OUNCES & GRAMS.

Avoirdupois Ounces	to	Grams	Grams	to	Avoirdupois Ounces
1 oz	....	28.35 g	1 g	....	.03 oz
2 oz	....	56.70 g	2 g	....	.07 oz
3 oz	....	85.05 g	3 g	....	.10 oz
4 oz	....	113.39 g	4 g	....	.14 oz
5 oz	....	141.74 g	5 g	....	.17 oz
6 oz	....	170.09 g	6 g	....	.21 oz
7 oz	....	198.44 g	7 g	....	.24 oz
8 oz	....	226.79 g	8 g	....	.28 oz
9 oz	....	255.14 g	9 g	....	.31 oz
10 oz	....	283.49 g	10 g	....	.35 oz
11 oz	....	311.48 g	11 g	....	.38 oz
12 oz	....	340.19 g	12 g	....	.42 oz
13 oz	....	368.54 g	13 g	....	.45 oz
14 oz	....	396.89 g	14 g	....	.49 oz
15 oz	....	425.24 g	15 g	....	.53 oz
16 oz (1 lb)	....	453.59 g	16 g	....	.56 oz
20 oz	....	566.99 g	20 g	....	.70 oz
30 oz	....	850.48 g	30 g	....	1.05 oz
40 oz	....	1133.98 g	40 g	....	1.41 oz
50 oz	....	1417.47 g	50 g	....	1.76 oz
60 oz	....	1700.97 g	60 g	....	2.11 oz
70 oz	....	1984.46 g	70 g	....	2.47 oz
80 oz	....	2267.96 g	80 g	....	2.82 oz
90 oz	....	2551.45 g	90 g	....	3.17 oz
100 oz	....	2834.95 g	100 g	....	3.52 oz

VOLUME CONVERSION FACTORS

TO CONVERT	TO	MULTIPLY BY	TO CONVERT	TO	MULTIPLY BY
teaspoons	milliliters	5	milliliters	teaspoons	0.2
tablespoons	milliliters	15	milliliters	tablespoons	0.6
fluid ounces	milliliters	29.57	milliliters	fluid ounces	0.03
cups	liters	0.24	milliliters	cups	0.004
pints	liters	0.47	liters	cups	0.42
quarts	liters	0.95	liters	pints	2.11
gallons	liters	3.78	liters	quarts	1.06
			liters	gallons	0.26

VOLUME CONVERSION CHARTS

5 milliliters	1 teaspoon		32 ounces	1 quart
15 milliliters	1 tablespoon		2 pints	1 quart
250 milliliters	1 cup		4 cups	1 quart
500 milliliters	1.06 pints		4 quarts	1 gallon
29.57 milliliters	1 fluid ounce		3 teaspoons	1 tablespoon
3.78 liters	1 gallon		16 tablespoons	1 cup
1 liter	1.06 quarts			
1 liter	2.11 pints			
1 liter	0.26 gallons			

MEASURING CUPS & SPOONS.

Teaspoons Tablespoons and Cups	to	Milli- liters	Milliliters	to	Cups
1 tsp		5 ml	100 ml		.4 c
2 tsp		10 ml	200 ml		.8 c
3 tsp (1 tbsp) ...		15 ml	300 ml		1.2 c
2 tbsp		30 ml	400 ml		1.6 c
3 tbsp		45 ml	500 ml		2.0 c
4 tbsp		60 ml	600 ml		2.4 c
5 tbsp		75 ml	700 ml		2.8 c
6 tbsp		90 ml	800 ml		3.2 c
7 tbsp		105 ml	900 ml		3.6 c
8 tbsp		120 ml	1000 ml ..... (1 qt)		4.0 c
9 tbsp		135 ml	1100 ml		4.4 c
10 tbsp		150 ml	1200 ml		4.8 c
11 tbsp		165 ml	1300 ml		5.2 c
12 tbsp		180 ml	1400 ml		5.6 c
13 tbsp		195 ml	1500 ml		6.0 c
14 tbsp		210 ml	1600 ml		6.4 c
15 tbsp		225 ml	1700 ml		6.8 c
16 tbsp (1 cup) ..		240 ml	1800 ml		7.2 c
2 c		480 ml	1900 ml		7.6 c
3 c		720 ml	2000 ml .... (½ gal)		8.0 c
4 c (1 qt)		960 ml	2100 m		8.4 c
8 c (½ gal)		1920 ml	2200 ml		8.8 c
12 c		2880 ml	2300 ml		9.2 c
16 c (1 gal)		3840 ml	2400 ml		9.6 c
32 c		7680 ml	2500 ml		10.0 c
80 c (5 gal)		19200 ml	2600 ml		10.4 c

146

GALLONS & LITERS.

Gallons to Liters	Liters to Gallons
1 gal .... 3.78 l	1 l ....0.26 gal
2 gal .... 7.57 l	2 l ....0.53 gal
3 gal ....11.36 l	3 l ....0.79 gal
4 gal ....15.14 l	4 l ....1.06 gal
5 gal ....18.93 l	5 l ....1.32 gal
6 gal ....22.71 l	6 l ....1.59 gal
7 gal ....26.50 l	7 l ....1.85 gal
8 gal ....30.28 l	8 l ....2.11 gal
9 gal ....34.07 l	9 l ....2.38 gal
10 gal ....37.85 l	10 l ....2.64 gal

FLUID QUARTS & LITERS.

Fluid Quarts to Liters	Fluid Liters to Quarts
1 qt ....0.95 l	1 l .... 1.06 qt
2 qt ....1.89 l	2 l .... 2.12 qt
3 qt ....2.84 l	3 l .... 3.17 qt
4 qt ....3.79 l	4 l .... 4.23 qt
5 qt ....4.73 l	5 l .... 5.28 qt
6 qt ....5.68 l	6 l .... 6.34 qt
7 qt ....6.62 l	7 l .... 7.40 qt
8 qt ....7.57 l	8 l .... 8.45 qt
9 qt ....8.52 l	9 l .... 9.51 qt
10 qt ....9.46 l	10 l ....10.57 qt

FLUID OUNCES & MILLILITERS.

Fluid Ounces to Milliliters	Fluid Milliliters to Ounces
1 oz .... 29.57 ml	1 ml .... .03 oz
2 oz .... 59.15 ml	2 ml .... .07 oz
3 oz .... 88.72 ml	3 ml .... .10 oz
4 oz ....118.29 ml	4 ml .... .14 oz
5 oz ....147.87 ml	5 ml .... .17 oz
6 oz ....177.44 ml	6 ml .... .20 oz
7 oz ....207.02 ml	7 ml .... .23 oz
8 oz ....236.59 ml	8 ml .... .27 oz
9 oz ....266.16 ml	9 ml .... .30 oz
10 oz ....295.73 ml	10 ml .... .33 oz
11 oz ....325.31 ml	11 ml .... .37 oz
12 oz ....354.88 ml	12 ml .... .41 oz
13 oz ....384.46 ml	13 ml .... .44 oz
14 oz ....414.03 ml	14 ml .... .47 oz
15 oz ....443.60 ml	15 ml .... .50 oz
16 oz ....473.18 ml	16 ml .... .54 oz
17 oz ....502.75 ml	17 ml .... .57 oz
18 oz ....532.32 ml	18 ml .... .61 oz
19 oz ....561.90 ml	19 ml .... .64 oz
20 oz ....591.47 ml	20 ml .... .68 oz
21 oz ....621.04 ml	21 ml .... .71 oz
22 oz ....650.62 ml	22 ml .... .74 oz
23 oz ....680.19 ml	23 ml .... .78 oz
24 oz ....709.77 ml	24 ml .... .81 oz
25 oz ....739.34 ml	25 ml .... .85 oz
26 oz ....768.91 ml	26 ml .... .88 oz
27 oz ....798.48 ml	27 ml .... .91 oz
28 oz ....828.06 ml	28 ml .... .95 oz
29 oz ....857.63 ml	29 ml .... .98 oz
30 oz ....887.21 ml	30 ml ....1.01 oz
31 oz ....916.78 ml	31 ml ....1.05 oz
32 oz (1 qt) ....946.35 ml	32 ml ....1.08 oz

Weights & Measures
(AND OVEN TEMPERATURES)

WEIGHTS AND MEASURES

Dash/	less than 1/8 teaspoon	1 Pound of flour/	4 cups
3 Teaspoons/	1 tablespoon	1 Pound of sugar	
2 tablespoons/	1 liquid ounce	(granulated)/	2 cups
4 Tablespoons/	1/4 cup	1 Pound of butter/	2 cups
8 Tablespoons/	1/2 cup	1 Stick of butter/	1/2 cup
12 Tablespoons/	3/4 cup		
16 Tablespoons/	1 cup		
1 Cup/	1/2 pint (liquid)		
2 Pints/	1 quart		
4 Quarts/	1 gallon		

CAN SIZES

8-oz. can/	1 cup, serves 2
No. 1 can/	1-1/4 cups, serves 3
No. 303 can/	2 cups, serves 4
No. 2 can/	2-1/2 cups, serves 6
No. 2-1/2 can/	3-1/2 cups, serves 7 or 8
No. 3 cylinder/	5-3/4 cups, serves 10 to 12

TEMPERATURE CONVERSION FACTORS

To convert Fahrenheit temperature to Celsius temperature subtract 32 from the Fahrenheit temperature and multiply by 5/9.

To convert Celsius temperature to Fahrenheit temperature multiply the Celsius temperature by 9/5 then add 32.

COOKING TEMPERATURES

32°	Freezes water
70° to 75°	Room temperature
85° to 100°	Lukewarm liquid for yeast
165° to 175°	Simmer
212°	Boils water at sea level
230° to 234°	Makes thread from syrup
234° to 240°	Makes soft ball from syrup
244° to 248°	Makes firm ball from syrup
250° to 266°	Makes hard ball from syrup
320°	Makes sugar liquid
338°	Makes liquid sugar caramalize
375° to 400°	Deep-fat frying
550°	Broiling

OVEN TEMPERATURES

FAHRENHEIT		CELSIUS
250° to 300°	Very slow	121°C—154°C
300° to 325°	Slow	154°C—163°C
325° to 350°	Moderate	163°C—177°C
375°	Moderately hot	191°C
400° to 425°	Hot	204°C—218°C
450° and over	Very hot	232°C

Cooking Hints

Ingredient Substitutions

ARROWROOT   1 tablespoon=2 tablespoons flour (as thickening).

BAKING POWDER   1 teaspoon=2/3 teaspoon double-action type or 1/4 teaspoon baking soda plus 1/2 teaspoon cream of tartar.

CHOCOLATE   1 ounce (1 square)=3 tablespoons cocoa plus 1 teaspoon to 1 tablespoon shortening (less for Dutch cocoa).

CORNSTARCH   1 tablespoon=2 tablespoons flour (for thickening).

FLOUR
PASTRY FLOUR   1 cup=1 cup all-purpose or bread flour less 2 tablespoons.
POTATO FLOUR   1 tablespoon=2 tablespoons flour (as thickening).

MILK
FRESH, WHOLE   1 cup=1/2 cup evaporated milk plus 1/2 cup water or 1/2 cup condensed milk plus 1/2 cup water (reduce the sugar in the recipe) or 1/4 cup powdered whole milk plus 1 cup water or 1/4 cup powdered skim milk plus 2 tablespoons butter and 1 cup water.

FRESH, SKIM   1 cup=1/4 cup powdered skim milk plus 1 cup water.

SOUR   1 cup=1 cup lukewarm fresh milk (less 1 tablespoon) plus 1 tablespoon vinegar. Let stand 5 mintues.

Cooking Definitions

BARD. To add fat to meat before roasting to keep it from drying out. Lay strips of fat salt pork, bacon or other fat on top of the meat. See also Lard (below).

BASTE. Moisten by spooning a liquid over a roast or other food as it cooks.

BLANCH. Dip in and out of boiling water to loosen the skins of fruit or nuts or to prepare food for freezing.

DREDGE. Coat with flour or sugar.

DUST. Sprinkly lightly with flour or sugar.

GLAZE. Cover with a thin coating of jelly, meat juices or caramel.

LARD. Have the butcher thread strips of fat salt pork through very lean meat. See also Bard (above).

MARINATE. Cover with a liquid (usually wine or a highly seasoned sauce) and let stand to season or become tender.

PARBOIL. Partially cook (usually in boiling water) in preparation for further cooking.

REDUCE. COOK a liquid until some has been carried off as steam.

SCALLOP. BAKE in a sauce with crumbs on top. Often with grated cheese as well.

SCORE. MAKE a series of shallow cuts on the surface of a food.

SEAR. COOK at high temperature over direct heat or in the oven until the surface is browned.

Personal Index

PAGE

PAGE

Guest Lists

OCCASION

DATE

GUESTS

OCCASION

DATE

GUESTS

OCCASION

DATE

GUESTS

OCCASION

DATE

GUESTS

Guest Lists

OCCASION

DATE

GUESTS

OCCASION

DATE

GUESTS

OCCASION

DATE

GUESTS

OCCASION

DATE

GUESTS

Guest Lists

OCCASION

DATE

GUESTS

OCCASION

DATE

GUESTS

OCCASION

DATE

GUESTS

OCCASION

DATE

GUESTS